EMBRACING NEURODIVERSITY

Understanding and Celebrating The Spectrum of Minds

Table of Contents

CHAPTER 1: INTRODUCTION TO THE CONCEPT OF NEURODIVERSITY

Neurodiversity is a term that has gained significant traction in recent years, yet its roots stretch far back into the fabric of human history. At its core, neurodiversity challenges the traditional notion of what constitutes "normal" cognitive functioning, advocating instead for the recognition and acceptance of the vast array of neurological differences that exist in the human population.

Neurodiversity encompasses the understanding that every individual's brain is unique, with its own strengths, weaknesses, and idiosyncrasies. From autism spectrum disorder (ASD) to attention deficit hyperactivity disorder (ADHD), dyslexia, dyspraxia, and beyond, neurodiversity acknowledges the rich tapestry of neurological variations that contribute to the diversity of human experience.

Neurodiversity is a celebration of the spectrum of minds that make up our world. Rather than viewing neurodivergent individuals as outliers or deviations from the norm, neurodiversity invites us to recognize their inherent value and contributions to society. It rejects the notion of pathology, instead reframing neurological differences as natural variations that have existed throughout human history.

The importance of understanding and embracing neurodiversity in today's society cannot be overstated. In an increasingly interconnected and diverse world, fostering inclusivity and acceptance of all individuals, regardless of neurology, is not only a moral imperative but also a practical necessity.

First and foremost, embracing neurodiversity promotes social justice and equity. Historically, neurodivergent individuals have faced discrimination, stigma, and marginalization due to a lack of understanding and acceptance of their differences. By challenging these entrenched attitudes and advocating for neurodiversity, we can work towards creating a more just and inclusive society where all individuals are valued and respected for who they are.

As well, neurodiversity fosters innovation and creativity. Many of the greatest breakthroughs in science, technology, art, and culture have been made by individuals whose minds operate outside of the typical neurotypical framework. By embracing neurodiversity, we open ourselves up to new perspectives, ideas, and ways of thinking that have the potential to revolutionize industries and drive progress forward.

Moreover, understanding neurodiversity is essential for creating supportive environments in education, employment, and healthcare. By recognizing the unique strengths and challenges of neurodivergent individuals, we can develop tailored interventions and accommodations that enable them to thrive in various settings. Whether it's providing alternative learning methods for neurodivergent students or implementing flexible work arrangements for neurodivergent employees, embracing neurodiversity benefits not only individuals but also society as a whole.

In addition, embracing neurodiversity promotes mental health and well-being. All too often, neurodivergent individuals face increased rates of anxiety, depression, and other mental health challenges due to societal stigma and lack of support. By fostering a culture of acceptance and understanding, we can help alleviate the psychological burden that many neurodivergent individuals carry and promote mental wellness for all.

In conclusion, neurodiversity is not just a concept—it's a movement towards a more compassionate, inclusive, and equitable society. By recognizing and embracing the diversity of neurological differences that exist within the human population, we can build a world where every individual is valued, celebrated, and empowered to reach their full potential. Embracing neurodiversity is not only the right thing to do—it's essential for creating a brighter and more inclusive future for all.

CHAPTER 2: HISTORICAL OVERVIEW OF NEURODIVERSITY

The concept of neurodiversity has deep roots that stretch back centuries, but it wasn't until relatively recently that it gained widespread recognition and acceptance. Understanding the historical context of neurodiversity sheds light on its evolution as a social and scientific movement.

The term "neurodiversity" was coined by Australian sociologist Judy Singer in the late 1990s, although its origins can be traced back to earlier work by individuals such as Harvey Blume and Jim Sinclair. However, the idea of neurodiversity itself predates the term, with historical figures exhibiting neurodivergent traits long before the concept was formally articulated.

Throughout history, neurodivergent individuals have often been misunderstood, marginalized, and stigmatized by society. From the witch hunts of the Middle Ages to the eugenics movement of the early 20th century, attitudes towards neurodiversity have been shaped by fear, ignorance, and prejudice.

Despite these challenges, there have always been pioneers and advocates who have championed the rights and dignity of neurodivergent individuals. One such figure is Temple Grandin, a renowned autism advocate and author who has helped to raise awareness about autism spectrum disorder and promote acceptance of neurodiversity.

Another influential figure in the neurodiversity movement is Lorna Wing, a British psychiatrist who played a key role in redefining our understanding of autism. Her research helped to challenge prevailing stereotypes and misconceptions about autism, paving the way for a more nuanced and compassionate approach to supporting autistic individuals.

In addition to individual advocates, there have been organizations and communities that have played a crucial role in advancing the neurodiversity movement. The Autism Rights Movement, for example, emerged in the 1990s as a grassroots effort to promote the rights and autonomy of autistic individuals. Similarly, the Neurodiversity Movement has sought to challenge the medical model of disability and promote the idea that neurological differences should be celebrated rather than pathologized.

Today, the neurodiversity movement continues to gain momentum, thanks in part to the efforts of pioneers and advocates who have worked tirelessly to raise awareness and promote acceptance of neurodivergent individuals.

While there is still much work to be done, the historical overview of neurodiversity reminds us of the progress that has been made and the importance of continuing to advocate for a more inclusive and equitable society for all.

CHAPTER 3: EXPLORING THE NEURODIVERSITY SPECTRUM

The neurodiversity spectrum is as vast and varied as the human experience itself, encompassing a wide range of neurological differences that shape how individuals perceive and interact with the world around them. From autism to ADHD to dyslexia and beyond, each neurodivergent condition brings its own unique strengths, challenges, and perspectives to the table.

Autism spectrum disorder (ASD) is perhaps one of the most well-known neurodivergent conditions, characterized by differences in social communication and interaction, as well as restricted and repetitive patterns of behavior and interests. (Moller, 2023) However, it's important to recognize that autism is not a one-size-fits-all diagnosis. The autism spectrum is incredibly diverse, with individuals exhibiting a wide range of abilities and characteristics. Some may excel in areas such as mathematics, music, or visual arts, while others may struggle with sensory sensitivities or social skills. By embracing the diversity within the autism spectrum, we can better support and celebrate the unique talents and perspectives of autistic individuals.

Attention deficit hyperactivity disorder (ADHD) is another common neurodivergent condition that affects millions of people worldwide. ADHD is characterized by difficulties with attention, hyperactivity, and impulsivity, but again, the spectrum of ADHD is broad and multifaceted. Some individuals with ADHD may struggle with organization and time management, while others may thrive in fast-paced, dynamic environments. By recognizing the diversity within the ADHD spectrum, we can tailor interventions and accommodations to meet the specific needs of each individual.

Dyslexia is a neurodevelopmental disorder that affects reading and language processing, but like autism and ADHD, dyslexia is not a monolithic condition. While some individuals with dyslexia may struggle with reading fluency and comprehension, others may excel in areas such as visual thinking, problem-solving, and creativity. By understanding the diversity within the dyslexia spectrum, we can provide targeted interventions and support to help dyslexic individuals harness their strengths and overcome challenges.

Beyond autism, ADHD, and dyslexia, the neurodiversity spectrum encompasses a wide range of other conditions, including dyspraxia, dyscalculia, Tourette syndrome, and more. Each of these conditions brings its own unique set of strengths and challenges, and each individual's experience is shaped by a complex interplay of genetic, environmental, and neurological factors.

In conclusion, exploring the neurodiversity spectrum is essential for understanding and appreciating the rich tapestry of human cognition and experience. By recognizing the diversity within each neurodivergent condition, we can move beyond stereotypes and stigma to embrace the unique talents, perspectives, and contributions of neurodivergent individuals. Embracing neurodiversity means celebrating the full spectrum of human diversity and creating a more inclusive and equitable society for all.

CHAPTER 4: BREAKING STEREOTYPES AND MISCONCEPTIONS

Neurodivergent individuals have long been the victims of stereotypes and misconceptions that stem from a lack of understanding and awareness about their unique experiences and perspectives. Breaking down these stereotypes and challenging misconceptions is essential for promoting acceptance and inclusion of neurodiversity in society.

One common misconception about neurodivergent individuals is that they are somehow "broken" or "less than" their neurotypical counterparts. This harmful stereotype perpetuates the idea that neurodivergence is a deficit rather than a natural variation in human cognition. In reality, neurodivergent individuals possess a diverse range of strengths, talents, and abilities that are often overlooked or undervalued by society.

CHAPTER 5: NEURODIVERSITY IN THE WORKPLACE

The inclusion of neurodivergent individuals in the workplace is a matter of social and strategic advantage and responsibility for businesses. Embracing neurodiversity in various industries can lead to a more innovative, productive, and inclusive work environment.

One of the key benefits of neurodiversity in the workplace is enhanced creativity and problem-solving. Neurodivergent individuals often possess unique perspectives and unconventional ways of thinking that can lead to breakthrough ideas and solutions. By harnessing the diverse talents and cognitive styles of neurodivergent employees, organizations can foster a culture of innovation and out-of-the-box thinking.

Moreover, neurodiversity can improve overall team dynamics and collaboration. By bringing together individuals with different strengths, skills, and perspectives, teams can complement each other's abilities and work more effectively towards common goals. Neurodivergent individuals may excel in areas such as attention to detail, pattern recognition, and logical reasoning, which can enhance the overall performance of the team. (Moller, Autism myths and stereotypes 2023 Neurodiversity and the Spectrum of Neurodevelopment Par.2)

Creating an inclusive work environment for neurodivergent individuals requires intentional efforts and strategies. One approach is to provide training and education for all employees to increase awareness and understanding of neurodiversity. By fostering a culture of empathy and respect, organizations can create an environment where neurodivergent individuals feel valued and supported.

Another strategy is to implement reasonable accommodations to ensure that neurodivergent employees have equal access to opportunities and resources. This may include providing flexible work arrangements, sensory-friendly workspaces, or assistive technologies to accommodate individual needs and preferences.

Additionally, fostering open communication and collaboration can help create a sense of belonging and community for neurodivergent employees. Encouraging feedback and participation from all team members can help ensure that everyone's voices are heard and respected.

Overall, embracing neurodiversity in the workplace is not only the right thing to do from a moral standpoint, but it also makes good business sense. By harnessing the diverse talents and perspectives of neurodivergent individuals, organizations can drive innovation, improve team dynamics, and create a more inclusive and equitable workplace for all.

CHAPTER 6: NEURODIVERSITY IN EDUCATION

Recognizing and accommodating the diverse learning styles of neurodivergent students is crucial for creating inclusive and effective educational environments. Understanding the unique needs and preferences of neurodivergent learners allows educators to implement strategies that support their academic success and overall well-being.

Neurodivergent students encompass a wide range of profiles, including those with autism spectrum disorder (ASD), attention deficit hyperactivity disorder (ADHD), dyslexia, dyspraxia, and other neurodevelopmental differences. Each of these conditions comes with its own set of strengths and challenges, requiring educators to adopt a flexible and individualized approach to teaching and learning.

One key aspect of neurodiversity in education is understanding the unique learning styles of neurodivergent students. While neurotypical learners may thrive in traditional classroom settings with lectures and written assignments, neurodivergent students often benefit from alternative teaching methods that accommodate their diverse needs and preferences.

For example, neurodivergent students may excel in hands-on, experiential learning activities that engage multiple senses and allow for exploration and discovery. Providing opportunities for kinesthetic learning, such as interactive experiments, projects, and role-playing activities, can help neurodivergent students better understand and retain information.

Moreover, many neurodivergent students may benefit from visual supports and aids to enhance comprehension and organization. Visual schedules, graphic organizers, and pictorial representations can help neurodivergent students navigate complex tasks and concepts, providing them with a clear and structured framework for learning.

In addition, incorporating technology into the classroom can be particularly beneficial for neurodivergent students. Assistive technologies, such as text-to-speech software, speech recognition software, and mind-mapping tools, can help level the playing field for students with reading, writing, or organizational difficulties.

Implementing inclusive teaching methods is essential for creating a supportive and accessible learning environment for all students, regardless of neurodivergence. This may involve providing additional time or accommodations for assignments and assessments, offering alternative formats for materials, or adjusting the pace and structure of lessons to meet individual needs.

Furthermore, fostering a culture of acceptance and understanding is key to promoting inclusivity in education. Educators can play a vital role in creating classroom environments where neurodivergent students feel valued, respected, and supported. This may involve promoting empathy and compassion among students, addressing misconceptions and stereotypes about neurodiversity, and encouraging peer support and collaboration.

In conclusion, neurodiversity in education is about recognizing and celebrating the unique strengths and perspectives of neurodivergent students. By understanding their diverse learning styles and implementing inclusive teaching methods, educators can create environments where all students can thrive academically, socially, and emotionally. Embracing neurodiversity in education not only benefits neurodivergent students but also enriches the learning experience for all students, fostering a more inclusive and equitable educational system.

CHAPTER 7: FAMILY PERSPECTIVES ON NEURODIVERSITY

Navigating neurodiversity within the family dynamic can present both challenges and opportunities for growth. Understanding and supporting neurodivergent family members is essential for building strong, supportive relationships and fostering a sense of belonging and acceptance within the family unit.

Supporting neurodivergent family members begins with education and awareness. Parents and caregivers play a crucial role in advocating for their neurodivergent children and ensuring that their unique needs are met. This may involve seeking out information about their child's specific neurodivergent condition, connecting with support groups and resources, and collaborating with healthcare professionals to develop individualized treatment and support plans.

Moreover, building strong and supportive family relationships requires open communication and empathy. Family members should strive to create a safe and accepting environment where neurodivergent individuals feel valued, understood, and respected. This may involve actively listening to their perspectives and experiences, validating their feelings, and offering unconditional love and support.

In addition to emotional support, practical assistance can also be invaluable for neurodivergent family members. This may include helping them navigate daily tasks and routines, helping with organization and time management, and advocating for accommodations and accommodations in various settings.

Furthermore, fostering a sense of belonging and inclusion within the family can have a positive impact on the well-being of neurodivergent individuals. Encouraging participation in family activities, celebrating their achievements and milestones, and actively involving them in decision-making processes can help reinforce their sense of identity and self-worth.

It's also important for family members to recognize and address their own biases and misconceptions about neurodiversity. Challenging stigma and promoting understanding within the family can help create a more supportive and inclusive environment for everyone.

In conclusion, family perspectives on neurodiversity play a crucial role in shaping the experiences and outcomes of neurodivergent individuals. By supporting and advocating for their neurodivergent family members, families can build stronger, more resilient relationships and create environments where all members feel valued, accepted, and empowered to thrive. Embracing neurodiversity within the family unit not only benefits neurodivergent individuals but also enriches the lives of everyone involved, fostering greater empathy, understanding, and compassion within the family dynamic.

CHAPTER 8: INTERSECTIONALITY AND NEURODIVERSITY

Understanding the intersectionality of neurodiversity is essential for recognizing the complex and multifaceted experiences of neurodivergent individuals. Intersectionality refers to the interconnected nature of social categorizations such as race, gender, sexuality, socioeconomic status, and disability, and how these intersect to shape individuals' lived experiences and identities. When considering neurodiversity, it's crucial to explore how various aspects of identity intersect with neurodivergence and how these intersections can influence an individual's experiences and access to resources and support.

RACE AND NEURODIVERSITY:

Race intersects with neurodiversity in profound ways, shaping the experiences and outcomes of neurodivergent individuals from diverse racial and ethnic backgrounds. People of color who are neurodivergent often face unique challenges, including systemic racism, cultural stigma, and barriers to accessing culturally competent healthcare and support services. Moreover, racial stereotypes and biases can compound the challenges faced by neurodivergent individuals of color, leading to increased marginalization and discrimination.

GENDER AND NEURODIVERSITY:

Gender identity also intersects with neurodiversity, influencing the ways in which neurodivergent individuals navigate societal expectations and norms. Gender diverse and transgender neurodivergent individuals may face heightened discrimination and marginalization due to the intersection of their gender identity and neurodivergence. They may also encounter challenges accessing gender-affirming healthcare and support services, further exacerbating their vulnerability to discrimination and social exclusion.

SOCIOECONOMIC STATUS AND NEURODIVERSITY:

Socioeconomic status plays a significant role in shaping not only non-neurodivergent individuals experiences but also of neurodivergent individuals, with economic privilege often providing access to resources and support services that are unavailable to those from marginalized socioeconomic backgrounds. Neurodivergent individuals from low-income households may face additional barriers to accessing diagnosis, treatment, and accommodations, further exacerbating disparities in educational and employment outcomes.

OTHER IDENTITIES AND NEURODIVERSITY:

In addition to race, gender, and socioeconomic status, other aspects of identity such as sexuality, disability, and immigration status can intersect with neurodiversity to shape individuals' experiences and access to support and resources. For example, LGBTQ+ neurodivergent individuals may face unique challenges related to identity acceptance, discrimination, and accessing affirming healthcare and support services. Similarly, neurodivergent individuals with disabilities may encounter barriers to accessibility and accommodation in both physical and social environments.

ADDRESSING UNIQUE CHALLENGES:

Addressing the unique challenges faced by neurodivergent individuals from marginalized communities requires a holistic and intersectional approach that recognizes the interconnected nature of social identities and experiences. This may involve advocating for policies and practices that promote equity and inclusion, increasing access to culturally competent healthcare and support services, and amplifying the voices and experiences of marginalized neurodivergent individuals in decision-making processes.

Furthermore, it's essential to center the experiences and needs of neurodivergent individuals from marginalized communities in discussions and initiatives aimed at promoting neurodiversity and inclusion. By acknowledging and addressing the intersecting forms of discrimination and marginalization faced by neurodivergent individuals, we can work towards creating a more equitable and inclusive society where all individuals are valued and supported, regardless of their intersecting identities.

CHAPTER 9: NEURODIVERSITY AND MENTAL HEALTH

The relationship between neurodiversity and mental health is complex and multifaceted, with neurodivergent individuals often facing unique challenges and vulnerabilities that can impact their mental well-being. Understanding this relationship is essential for developing effective strategies to support the mental health needs of neurodivergent individuals and promote overall well-being.

EXPLORING THE LINK BETWEEN NEURODIVERGENCE AND MENTAL HEALTH CONDITIONS:

Neurodivergent individuals are more likely to experience mental health conditions compared to the general population. For example, studies have shown that individuals with autism spectrum disorder (ASD) are at increased risk for anxiety, depression, and other mood disorders (Hollocks et al., 2019). Similarly, individuals with attention deficit hyperactivity disorder (ADHD) may experience higher rates of anxiety and depression, as well as difficulties with emotion regulation and impulse control (Nigg, 2013).

The link between neurodivergence and mental health conditions can be attributed to various factors, including differences in neurobiology, sensory processing, social communication, and coping mechanisms. Neurodivergent individuals may also face additional stressors and challenges related to stigma, discrimination, and social isolation, which can and have contributed to the development of mental additional health issues. (Hirvikoski et al., 2016).

STRATEGIES FOR PROMOTING MENTAL WELL-BEING AMONG NEURODIVERGENT INDIVIDUALS:

Promoting mental well-being among neurodivergent individuals requires a holistic approach that addresses their unique needs and vulnerabilities.

1. Early Intervention and Screening: Early identification and intervention can help address mental health issues before they escalate. Routine screening for mental health conditions, particularly among neurodivergent individuals, can facilitate timely access to support and treatment (Hollocks et al., 2019).

2. Individualized Support: Providing individualized support tailored to the specific needs and preferences of neurodivergent individuals can promote their mental well-

being. This may include access to therapy, counseling, or support groups that address their unique challenges and strengths.

3. Skill-building and Coping Strategies: Teaching coping strategies and emotional regulation skills can empower neurodivergent individuals to manage stress and navigate social situations more effectively. Cognitive-behavioral therapy (CBT) and mindfulness-based interventions have shown promise in improving mental health outcomes for neurodivergent individuals (Hirvikoski et al., 2016).

4. Creating Supportive Environments: Creating supportive and inclusive environments in schools, workplaces, and communities can help reduce stigma and promote acceptance of neurodiversity. Educating others about neurodiversity and fostering empathy and understanding can contribute to a more inclusive and supportive culture.

5. Access to Resources and Services: Ensuring equitable access to mental health resources and services is essential for neurodivergent individuals. This includes access to affordable and culturally competent care, as well as accommodations and support services that address their unique needs.

In conclusion, addressing the link between neurodivergence and mental health is essential for promoting the well-being of neurodivergent individuals. By implementing strategies that support early intervention, individualized support, skill-building, creating supportive environments, and ensuring access to resources and services, we can empower neurodivergent individuals to thrive and lead fulfilling lives.

CHAPTER 10: ADVOCACY AND ACTIVISM IN THE NEURODIVERSITY MOVEMENT

The neurodiversity movement is fueled by the tireless efforts of advocates and activists who work to promote understanding, acceptance, and inclusion of neurodivergent individuals in all aspects of society. From grassroots organizations to influential individuals, the neurodiversity movement is driven by a diverse and dedicated community of changemakers who are driving positive change and challenging stigma and discrimination.

HIGHLIGHTING ORGANIZATIONS AND INDIVIDUALS DRIVING POSITIVE CHANGE:

1. Autistic Self Advocacy Network (ASAN): ASAN is a leading advocacy organization run by and for autistic individuals. They work to advance the rights and inclusion of autistic people in society through policy advocacy, community building, and public education.

2. Neurodiversity in the Workplace: Organizations like Neurodiversity in the Workplace advocate for inclusive hiring practices and support neurodivergent individuals in finding meaningful employment opportunities.

3. The Thinking Person's Guide to Autism: This online resource provides evidence-based information, support, and advocacy tools for autistic individuals, families, and professionals.

4. Temple Grandin: Renowned autism advocate Temple

Grandin has dedicated her life to raising awareness and promoting acceptance of autism spectrum disorder. Through her writing, speaking engagements, and advocacy work, she has inspired countless individuals and families.

5. Autistic Women & Nonbinary Network (AWN): AWN is dedicated to empowering and supporting autistic women, girls, and nonbinary individuals through advocacy, education, and community-building initiatives.

Ways to Get Involved and Support the Neurodiversity Community:

- Educate Yourself: Take the time to learn about neurodiversity, including different neurodivergent conditions and the experiences of neurodivergent individuals. Read books, watch documentaries, and listen to podcasts by neurodivergent authors and advocates.

- Support Neurodivergent-Owned Businesses: Seek out and support businesses owned and operated by neurodivergent individuals. This can include purchasing products or services from neurodivergent entrepreneurs or patronizing neurodivergent artists and creators.

- Amplify Neurodivergent Voices: Share and amplify the voices and perspectives of neurodivergent individuals. Follow neurodivergent activists and advocates on social media, share their content, and engage in conversations about neurodiversity and inclusion.

- Advocate for Inclusive Policies: Advocate for policies and practices that promote inclusion and accommodation for neurodivergent individuals in schools, workplaces, and communities. This can include supporting initiatives for inclusive education, accessible healthcare, and equitable employment opportunities.

- Volunteer with Neurodiversity Organizations: Get involved with organizations and initiatives that support neurodiversity advocacy and activism. Volunteer your time, skills, or resources to support their work and make a positive impact in the neurodiversity community.

By getting involved and supporting the neurodiversity movement, we can all play a role in creating a more inclusive, equitable, and compassionate society where neurodivergent individuals are valued, respected, and empowered to thrive.

CHAPTER 11: NEURODIVERSITY IN POPULAR CULTURE

Neurodiversity in popular culture is gaining recognition as media and literature increasingly feature diverse and nuanced representations of neurodivergent characters. From movies and television shows to novels and comics, the portrayal of neurodivergent individuals is challenging stereotypes and fostering greater understanding and acceptance within society.

The representation of neurodivergent characters in popular culture is diverse, spanning a wide range of genres and mediums. Characters with autism, ADHD, dyslexia, and other neurodivergent traits are depicted as multifaceted individuals with unique strengths, challenges, and experiences.

Accurate representation of neurodivergent characters in media and literature has a profound impact on societal attitudes towards neurodiversity. By portraying neurodivergent characters in a positive and authentic light, popular culture helps to challenge stereotypes, break down stigma, and promote empathy and understanding among audiences.

When neurodivergent characters are portrayed with complexity and humanity, audiences are given the opportunity to connect with their experiences on a deeper level. This can lead to increased awareness and acceptance of neurodiversity, ultimately contributing to a more inclusive and compassionate society.

Moreover, accurate representation in popular culture has the power to empower neurodivergent individuals and validate their identities. Seeing characters who share their neurodivergent traits depicted in a positive and affirming manner can provide a sense of validation and belonging for neurodivergent individuals, helping to combat feelings of isolation and marginalization.

In conclusion, neurodiversity in popular culture plays a vital role in shaping societal attitudes towards neurodivergent individuals. By featuring diverse and authentic representations of neurodivergent characters, media and literature have the power to challenge stereotypes, promote empathy and understanding, and foster greater acceptance of neurodiversity within society.

CHAPTER 12: NEURODIVERSITY AND CREATIVITY

Neurodiversity and creativity often go hand in hand, with many neurodivergent individuals possessing unique perspectives, talents, and ways of thinking that fuel their creative endeavors. Exploring the intersection of neurodiversity and creativity highlights the rich diversity of human cognition and the immense contributions of neurodivergent artists, writers, and innovators to the arts and sciences.

Neurodivergent individuals often approach creativity in unconventional and innovative ways, drawing inspiration from their heightened sensory experiences, intense focus, and divergent thinking patterns. Their ability to see the world from different angles and make unexpected connections can lead to groundbreaking insights and artistic expressions that challenge norms and captivate audiences.

Examples of neurodivergent artists, writers, and innovators abound across history and contemporary culture. Temple Grandin, a renowned autism advocate and animal behavior expert, revolutionized the livestock industry with her humane livestock handling designs. Her unique perspective as an autistic individual informed her innovative approach to animal welfare.

Another example is artist and writer Hannah Gadsby, whose stand-up comedy special "Nanette" garnered critical acclaim for its raw honesty and vulnerability. Gadsby's experience as an autistic lesbian woman informs her storytelling, offering audiences a glimpse into her unique worldview and lived experiences.

In the world of literature, authors like Daniel Tammet, whose memoir "Born on a Blue Day" offers a vivid portrayal of life with synesthesia and Asperger's syndrome, showcase the power of neurodivergent voices in storytelling. Tammet's ability to vividly describe his sensory experiences and inner world captivates readers and challenges perceptions of neurodiversity.

In the arts, artists such as Stephen Wiltshire, known as the "human camera" for his extraordinary ability to accurately draw cityscapes from memory, demonstrate the remarkable talents of neurodivergent individuals. Wiltshire's hyper-realistic drawings offer a glimpse into his exceptional visual memory and attention to detail, showcasing the intersection of neurodiversity and artistic brilliance.

These examples underscore the immense creativity and talent present within the neurodivergent community. By embracing neurodiversity and recognizing the unique perspectives and talents of neurodivergent individuals, we can foster a more inclusive and innovative society that celebrates the diversity of human cognition and creativity.

CHAPTER 13: NEURODIVERSITY AND RELATIONSHIPS

Navigating relationships, whether friendships or romantic partnerships, can present unique challenges for neurodivergent individuals. Understanding the dynamics of neurodiversity in relationships is essential for fostering meaningful connections and promoting empathy and understanding among all parties involved.

Neurodivergent individuals may approach friendships, romantic relationships, and social interactions in ways that differ from neurotypical individuals. They may struggle with social cues, communication, and sensory sensitivities, which can impact their ability to form and maintain relationships. However, with understanding and support, neurodivergent individuals can cultivate fulfilling and meaningful connections with others.

In friendships, neurodivergent individuals may benefit

from clear communication, consistency, and patience from their friends. Understanding and respecting their boundaries, preferences, and sensory needs can help foster a supportive and inclusive friendship dynamic. Additionally, providing opportunities for shared interests and activities can strengthen the bond between neurodivergent individuals and their friends.

In romantic relationships, open communication, mutual respect, and empathy are essential for building a strong and healthy partnership. Neurodivergent individuals may appreciate partners who are patient, understanding, and willing to accommodate their unique needs and differences. Creating a safe and accepting space where both partners feel valued and supported can foster intimacy and trust within the relationship.

Tips for Building Meaningful Connections with Neurodivergent Individuals:

1. Practice Active Listening: Take the time to listen attentively to neurodivergent individuals, validating their experiences and perspectives. Show empathy and understanding by acknowledging their feelings and concerns without judgment.

2. Be Patient and Flexible: Understand that neurodivergent individuals may require additional time or support to process information or navigate social situations. Be patient and flexible in your interactions, allowing space for them to communicate at their own pace.

3. Respect Boundaries and Preferences: Respect the boundaries, preferences, and sensory needs of

neurodivergent individuals. Ask for consent before initiating physical contact or engaging in activities that may be overwhelming or uncomfortable for them.

4. Provide Clear Communication: Use clear and concise language when communicating with neurodivergent individuals, avoiding ambiguity or sarcasm. Be explicit about your intentions, expectations, and boundaries to avoid misunderstandings.

5. Celebrate Differences: Embrace the unique perspectives, talents, and strengths of neurodivergent individuals. Celebrate their achievements and contributions, recognizing the valuable insights and creativity they bring to relationships and social interactions.

By incorporating these tips and strategies into your interactions with neurodivergent individuals, you can build meaningful connections based on understanding, respect, and empathy. Ultimately, fostering inclusive and supportive relationships benefits everyone involved, enriching the lives of neurodivergent individuals, and promoting greater acceptance and appreciation of neurodiversity within society.

CHAPTER 14: NEURODIVERSITY AND SELF-ADVOCACY

Empowering neurodivergent individuals to advocate for their needs and rights is crucial for fostering independence, self-confidence, and inclusion. Self-advocacy involves recognizing one's strengths and challenges, articulating one's needs, and preferences, and actively participating in decision-making processes that affect one's life.

Research shows that self-advocacy skills are essential for neurodivergent individuals to navigate various settings, including education, employment, healthcare, and social interactions (Doren et al., 2012). By developing effective self-advocacy strategies, neurodivergent individuals can assert their rights, access accommodations and support services, and advocate for greater inclusivity and acceptance within society.

Strategies for self-advocacy in various settings include:

1. Know Yourself: Take the time to understand your strengths, challenges, and preferences. Reflect on your needs and goals and identify areas where you may require support or accommodations.

2. Educate Yourself: Learn about your rights and entitlements under relevant laws and policies, such as the Americans with Disabilities Act (ADA) or the Individuals with Disabilities Education Act (IDEA). Stay informed about available resources and support services in your community.

3. Communicate Effectively: Practice assertive communication skills, clearly articulating your needs, preferences, and boundaries. Be confident in expressing yourself and advocating for accommodations or adjustments that meet your needs.

4. Build a Support Network: Surround yourself with allies, advocates, and mentors who can offer guidance, encouragement, and support. Seek out peer support groups or online communities where you can connect with others who share similar experiences.

5. Stay Organized: Keep records of important documents, such as evaluations, assessments, and accommodation plans. Maintain a calendar or planner to track appointments, deadlines, and tasks related to your advocacy efforts.

By equipping neurodivergent individuals with self-advocacy skills, we can empower them to navigate challenges, access resources, and advocate for their rights and needs effectively. Cultivating a culture of self-advocacy not only benefits neurodivergent individuals but also promotes greater autonomy, empowerment, and inclusivity within society.

CHAPTER 15: NEURODIVERSITY AND IDENTITY

Neurodiversity is an integral aspect of identity for many individuals, encompassing a diverse range of cognitive styles, strengths, and challenges. Embracing neurodivergence as a fundamental aspect of identity involves recognizing and celebrating the unique perspectives and contributions of neurodivergent individuals to society.

For many neurodivergent individuals, their neurodivergent identity shapes their worldview, experiences, and interactions with the world around them. Rather than viewing neurodivergence as a deficit or limitation, embracing neurodivergence as a core aspect of identity reframes it as a natural variation in human cognition, deserving of acceptance and celebration.

Celebrating the unique strengths and perspectives of neurodivergent individuals is essential for promoting inclusivity, diversity, and equity within society. Neurodivergent individuals often possess exceptional talents and abilities, including heightened creativity, attention to detail, pattern recognition, and problem-solving skills. By recognizing and celebrating these strengths, we can challenge stereotypes and misconceptions about neurodiversity and foster greater appreciation for the diversity of human cognition.

Moreover, embracing neurodiversity as a fundamental aspect of identity encourages self-acceptance and empowerment among neurodivergent individuals. It validates their lived experiences, identities, and contributions, affirming their worth and value as equal members of society. This sense of validation and belonging is essential for promoting mental well-being, resilience, and self-confidence among neurodivergent individuals.

In conclusion, neurodiversity is an integral aspect of identity that shapes the experiences and perspectives of neurodivergent individuals. Embracing neurodivergence as a fundamental aspect of identity involves celebrating the unique strengths and contributions of neurodivergent individuals and challenging stigma and discrimination within society. By fostering a culture of acceptance, inclusivity, and celebration of neurodiversity, we can create a more equitable and compassionate world where all individuals are valued and respected for who they are.

CHAPTER 16: NEURODIVERSITY AND INNOVATION

Neurodiversity is increasingly recognized as a driving force behind innovation and creativity, with neurodivergent individuals often making significant contributions to groundbreaking discoveries and inventions across various fields. Understanding how neurodiversity fuels innovation sheds light on the unique perspectives and talents of neurodivergent individuals and highlights the importance of embracing diversity in driving progress and advancement.

Neurodivergent individuals often possess unconventional ways of thinking, problem-solving skills, and a keen attention to detail that can lead to innovative breakthroughs. Their ability to see patterns, make connections, and think outside the box can result in novel solutions to complex problems, driving innovation forward.

Research has shown that neurodivergent individuals, including those with autism, ADHD, dyslexia, and other neurodevelopmental differences, are overrepresented among inventors, entrepreneurs, and creative professionals (Happe & Vital, 2009). For example, individuals with autism are known for their exceptional attention to detail, intense focus, and ability to hyperfocus on specific topics of interest, qualities that are highly conducive to innovation and discovery.

Examples of groundbreaking discoveries and inventions by neurodivergent individuals abound across history and contemporary culture. One notable example is the work of Nikola Tesla, a renowned inventor and electrical engineer known for his contributions to the development of alternating current (AC) electricity. Tesla, who is believed to have had traits associated with neurodivergence, revolutionized the field of electrical engineering with his innovative ideas and inventions.

Another example is the work of Temple Grandin, an autistic animal behavior expert whose groundbreaking designs and innovations in livestock handling revolutionized the agricultural industry. Grandin's unique perspective as an autistic individual informed her innovative approach to animal welfare, resulting in more humane and efficient livestock handling practices.

Furthermore, neurodivergent individuals have made significant contributions to fields such as technology, engineering, mathematics, and the arts. Their unconventional thinking, creative problem-solving skills, and ability to see the world from different angles have led to breakthroughs and advancements that have shaped the course of human history.

In conclusion, neurodiversity is a driving force behind innovation and creativity, with neurodivergent individuals making significant contributions to groundbreaking discoveries and inventions across various fields. By embracing neurodiversity and recognizing the unique perspectives and talents of neurodivergent individuals, we can foster a culture of innovation, inclusivity, and progress that benefits society as a whole.

CHAPTER 17: NEURODIVERSITY AND SOCIETY

Neurodiversity plays a significant role in shaping culture, technology, and society, contributing to innovation, creativity, and progress. Recognizing and embracing neurodiversity is essential for building a more inclusive and equitable world that values the diversity of human cognition and experiences.

In culture, neurodiversity enriches artistic expression, literature, and media by offering unique perspectives and narratives that challenge norms and broaden understanding. Neurodivergent artists, writers, and creators bring their distinct voices and talents to the forefront, creating works that resonate with diverse audiences and foster empathy and acceptance.

In technology, neurodiversity drives innovation and advancement by bringing diverse perspectives and problem-solving skills to the table. Neurodivergent individuals often excel in fields such as science, technology, engineering, and mathematics (STEM), making significant contributions to research, development, and technological breakthroughs that benefit society as a whole.

In society, embracing neurodiversity promotes inclusivity, diversity, and equity by recognizing the value and contributions of all individuals, regardless of neurocognitive differences. Creating environments that accommodate and celebrate neurodiversity fosters a sense of belonging and empowerment among neurodivergent individuals, promoting their well-being and participation in social, educational, and employment opportunities.

Building a more inclusive and equitable world for all individuals requires dismantling stigma, discrimination, and barriers to access and participation. By promoting awareness, understanding, and acceptance of neurodiversity, we can create communities and institutions that embrace diversity, foster empathy, and empower all individuals to thrive and contribute their unique talents and perspectives to society.

In conclusion, neurodiversity plays a vital role in shaping culture, technology, and society, contributing to innovation, creativity, and progress. Embracing neurodiversity is essential for building a more inclusive and equitable world that values the diversity of human cognition and experiences, promoting empathy, acceptance, and empowerment for all individuals.

CHAPTER 18: NEURODIVERSITY AND HEALTHCARE: IMPROVING ACCESS AND ADDRESSING DISPARITIES

Neurodiversity profoundly influences healthcare, presenting unique challenges and disparities in diagnosis and treatment for neurodivergent individuals. Improving access to healthcare services and addressing these disparities are essential steps towards providing equitable and inclusive care for all.

Improving Access to Healthcare Services:

Accessing healthcare services can be daunting for neurodivergent individuals due to various barriers, including sensory sensitivities, communication difficulties, and a lack of provider understanding. To enhance access, healthcare systems must adopt inclusive practices that accommodate the diverse needs of neurodivergent patients.

Creating sensory-friendly healthcare environments, offering alternative communication methods (such as visual schedules or communication boards), and providing patient-centered care approaches are crucial steps towards improving access for neurodivergent individuals (Nicolaidis et al., 2011).

Addressing Disparities in Diagnosis and Treatment:

Disparities in the diagnosis and treatment of neurodivergent conditions contribute to inequalities in healthcare outcomes. Biases, limited diagnostic criteria, and cultural differences, can result in underdiagnosis, misdiagnosis, or delayed diagnosis for neurodivergent individuals.

Addressing these disparities requires healthcare providers to receive training in recognizing and understanding neurodiversity, including its manifestations across different populations. Culturally competent approaches to diagnosis and treatment are vital to ensure that neurodivergent individuals receive accurate assessments and appropriate interventions.

Equitable access to treatment options and support services is also essential for addressing disparities in healthcare outcomes. This includes ensuring affordability, availability, and accessibility of interventions such as behavioral therapies, assistive technologies, and educational accommodations.

Promoting Inclusive Healthcare Practices:

Promoting inclusive healthcare practices involves creating environments that are welcoming, respectful, and responsive to the needs of neurodivergent individuals. Collaboration between healthcare providers, educators, researchers, and advocacy organizations is essential for developing and implementing inclusive healthcare practices.

By working together, stakeholders can identify and address systemic barriers to care, advocate for policy changes, and promote awareness and understanding of neurodiversity within healthcare settings (Dabelea et al., 2014).

In conclusion, improving access to healthcare services for neurodivergent individuals requires a comprehensive approach that addresses barriers to care, disparities in diagnosis and treatment, and promotes inclusive healthcare practices. By recognizing and accommodating the diverse needs of neurodivergent patients, healthcare systems can provide more equitable and effective care for all.

CHAPTER 19: NEURODIVERSITY AND POLICY: ADVOCATING FOR INCLUSIVITY AND SUPPORT

Neurodiversity intersects with policy in significant ways, influencing the development of legislation and initiatives aimed at promoting inclusivity, accessibility, and support for neurodivergent individuals. Advocating for policies that prioritize the needs and rights of neurodivergent individuals is essential for creating a more equitable and inclusive society.

ADVOCATING FOR POLICIES THAT PROMOTE INCLUSIVITY:

Advocacy efforts focused on promoting inclusivity for neurodivergent individuals encompass a wide range of policy areas, including education, employment, healthcare, and social services. These efforts aim to address systemic barriers, discrimination, and disparities faced by neurodivergent individuals and ensure their full participation and integration into society.

Policies promoting inclusive education seek to provide neurodivergent students with access to appropriate accommodations, support services, and educational opportunities that meet their diverse needs. This may include implementing universal design principles in curriculum development, providing assistive technologies, and fostering inclusive classroom environments that celebrate neurodiversity.

In the realm of employment, policies promoting neurodiversity in the workplace aim to create inclusive hiring practices, provide reasonable accommodations, and support career development for neurodivergent individuals. Initiatives such as job training programs, mentorship opportunities, and workplace diversity initiatives can help remove barriers to employment and promote workplace inclusivity.

EXAMPLES OF SUCCESSFUL POLICY INITIATIVES:

1. The Americans with Disabilities Act (ADA): Enacted in 1990, the ADA prohibits discrimination against individuals with disabilities in all areas of public life, including employment, education, transportation, and public accommodations. The ADA has played a crucial role in promoting inclusivity and accessibility for neurodivergent individuals by requiring reasonable accommodations and ensuring equal opportunities in various settings.

2. Individuals with Disabilities Education Act (IDEA): IDEA is a federal law that ensures students with disabilities, including neurodivergent students, receive a free and appropriate public education tailored to their unique needs. IDEA mandates the provision of special education services, accommodations, and supports to eligible students, promoting inclusivity and access to educational opportunities for neurodivergent individuals.

3. Autism CARES Act: The Autism Collaboration, Accountability, Research, Education, and Support (CARES) Act, originally enacted in 2006 and reauthorized in

2019, provides funding for autism research, surveillance, education, and early intervention services. The Act aims to improve access to diagnostic services, support evidence-based interventions, and promote interdisciplinary research collaborations, advancing understanding and support for individuals with autism spectrum disorder (ASD).

These examples highlight the importance of policy initiatives in promoting inclusivity, accessibility, and support for neurodivergent individuals. By advocating for policies that prioritize the needs and rights of neurodivergent individuals, we can create a more equitable and inclusive society that celebrates and embraces neurodiversity.

CHAPTER 20: NEURODIVERSITY AND THE FUTURE: ENVISIONING A CELEBRATED AND VALUED WORLD

As we look towards the future, embracing neurodiversity holds the promise of creating a more inclusive, innovative, and compassionate society. By recognizing and celebrating the diverse range of neurocognitive profiles and experiences, we can unlock the full potential of all individuals and pave the way for a brighter future for generations to come.

THE POTENTIAL IMPACT OF EMBRACING NEURODIVERSITY:

Embracing neurodiversity has the potential to revolutionize various aspects of society, including education, employment, healthcare, and culture. By recognizing and accommodating the unique strengths, perspectives, and talents of neurodivergent individuals, we can foster greater creativity, collaboration, and innovation across all sectors.

In education, embracing neurodiversity means moving away from one-size-fits-all approaches to learning and adopting more inclusive and personalized educational practices. By recognizing and supporting diverse learning styles and needs, we can create learning environments that empower all students to succeed and thrive.

In employment, embracing neurodiversity means promoting inclusive hiring practices, providing reasonable accommodations, and creating supportive work environments that value diversity and inclusion. By tapping into the unique skills and perspectives of neurodivergent individuals, businesses and organizations can drive innovation, productivity, and success.

In healthcare, embracing neurodiversity means ensuring equitable access to quality care and support services for neurodivergent individuals. By addressing disparities in diagnosis and treatment, promoting awareness, and understanding of neurodiversity among healthcare providers, and adopting inclusive healthcare practices, we can improve health outcomes and well-being for all.

ENVISIONING A WORLD WHERE NEURODIVERSITY IS CELEBRATED AND VALUED:

In a world where neurodiversity is celebrated and valued, individuals of all neurocognitive profiles are recognized and respected for their unique contributions and perspectives. In this world, differences are not seen as deficits but as strengths, and diversity is embraced as a source of richness and innovation.

Schools are inclusive and accommodating, providing personalized learning experiences that cater to the diverse needs and strengths of every student. Workplaces are diverse and supportive, fostering environments where all employees feel valued, respected, and empowered to contribute their best.

Healthcare systems are equitable and accessible, providing comprehensive care and support services that address the diverse needs of neurodivergent individuals across the lifespan. Stigma and discrimination against neurodivergent individuals are replaced with empathy, acceptance, and understanding.

In this world, neurodiversity is not just tolerated but celebrated as a fundamental aspect of human diversity. By embracing neurodiversity and fostering a culture of inclusivity and acceptance, we can create a world where all individuals are valued, supported, and empowered to reach their full potential.

In conclusion, embracing neurodiversity holds the key to creating a more inclusive, innovative, and compassionate society. By recognizing and celebrating the diverse range of neurocognitive profiles and experiences, we can envision a future where neurodiversity is celebrated and valued, paving the way for a brighter and more equitable world for generations to come.

CHAPTER 21: CONCLUSION: EMBRACING NEURODIVERSITY IN OUR JOURNEY FORWARD

As we conclude our exploration of neurodiversity, it is essential to reflect on the journey we have embarked on and reaffirm our commitment to promoting understanding, acceptance, and celebration of neurodiversity in our lives and communities. The significance of embracing neurodiversity extends far beyond the pages of this book—it is a continuous journey towards building a more inclusive, empathetic, and equitable society for all.

Reflecting on the Journey Through Neurodiversity:

Our journey through neurodiversity has been enlightening, challenging, and transformative. We have explored the diverse range of neurocognitive profiles and experiences that make up the fabric of human diversity, recognizing the unique strengths, challenges, and contributions of neurodivergent individuals. We have learned about the importance of challenging stereotypes, addressing stigma, and advocating for policies and practices that promote inclusivity and support for neurodivergent individuals across all aspects of society.

Throughout this journey, we have encountered stories of resilience, creativity, and perseverance, as neurodivergent individuals navigate a world that often fails to understand and accommodate their unique needs. We have witnessed the power of empathy, acceptance, and allyship in creating spaces where neurodiversity is celebrated and valued, fostering a sense of belonging and empowerment for all individuals.

THE IMPORTANCE OF CONTINUING TO PROMOTE UNDERSTANDING AND ACCEPTANCE:

As we conclude our exploration of neurodiversity, it is crucial to recognize that our journey is far from over. The work of promoting understanding and acceptance of neurodiversity must continue, both at the individual and societal levels. We must challenge ourselves to confront biases, dismantle barriers, and advocate for policies and practices that promote inclusivity, accessibility, and support for neurodivergent individuals in all areas of life.

By continuing to promote understanding and acceptance of neurodiversity, we can create communities and institutions that celebrate diversity, foster empathy, and empower all individuals to thrive and contribute their unique talents and perspectives to society. This requires ongoing education, dialogue, and action to break down stereotypes, address stigma, and create environments where neurodiversity is embraced as a source of strength and innovation.

Encouragement for Readers to Embrace Neurodiversity:

As we conclude our journey through neurodiversity, I encourage readers to embrace neurodiversity in their own lives and communities. Take the time to learn about the diverse experiences and perspectives of neurodivergent individuals, listen to their stories, and amplify their voices. Challenge stereotypes, advocate for inclusivity, and create spaces where all individuals feel valued, respected, and supported.

Whether you are a parent, educator, healthcare provider, employer, or community member, you have the power to make a difference in promoting, understanding, and acceptance, of neurodiversity. Embrace diversity, celebrate differences, and work towards building a world where everyone can thrive and reach their full potential, regardless of neurocognitive differences.

In conclusion, our journey through neurodiversity has been a testament to the power of empathy, acceptance, and advocacy in creating a more inclusive and equitable society. As we continue our path forward, let us reaffirm our commitment to promoting understanding and acceptance of neurodiversity, and embrace the richness and diversity of the human experience in all its forms. Together, we can build a world where neurodiversity is celebrated and valued, and all individuals are empowered to live their lives to the fullest.

CHAPTER 22: ADDITIONAL RESOURCES, HELP, AND HOTLINES, FOR FURTHER EXPLORATION OF NEURODIVERSITY

I want to dedicate this short book to my Friends, Family, and Community Members who struggle with Neurodiversity but continue to walk strong in the face of adversity and hardships. As we conclude our journey through the exploration of neurodiversity, it is essential to provide all readers with additional resources for further reading, support, and assistance.

Whether you are seeking to deepen your understanding of neurodiversity, connect with organizations and support groups, or access immediate assistance, the following resources offer valuable information and support for neurodivergent individuals, their families, and allies.

BOOKS:

1. "NeuroTribes: The Legacy of Autism and the Future of Neurodiversity" by Steve Silberman - This groundbreaking book provides a comprehensive history of autism and the neurodiversity movement, exploring the contributions of neurodivergent individuals to society.

2. "Uniquely Human: A Different Way of Seeing Autism" by Barry M. Prizant - Drawing on his decades of experience as a clinical psychologist, Prizant offers a compassionate and insightful perspective on autism, emphasizing the importance of understanding and embracing neurodiversity.

3. "The Autistic Brain: Helping Different Kinds of Minds Succeed" by Temple Grandin and Richard Panek - Temple Grandin, a prominent advocate for autism awareness, offers a fascinating exploration of the autistic brain and provides practical advice for supporting neurodivergent individuals.

ARTICLES AND WEBSITES:

1. Autism Speaks (www.autismspeaks.org) - Autism Speaks is a leading autism advocacy organization that offers resources, support, and information for individuals with autism spectrum disorder (ASD) and their families.

2. Neurodiversity Hub (www.neurodiversityhub.org) - The Neurodiversity Hub is an online platform that promotes awareness, acceptance, and understanding of neurodiversity through articles, videos, and resources.

3. The Aspergian (www.theaspergian.com) - The Aspergian is an online publication that amplifies the voices of neurodivergent individuals, offering insightful articles, personal essays, and creative works.

Organizations and Support Groups:

1. The Autistic Self Advocacy Network (ASAN) - ASAN is a grassroots organization run by and for autistic individuals, advocating for the rights and inclusion of neurodivergent

individuals in all aspects of society

2. The National Alliance on Mental Illness (NAMI) - NAMI provides support, education, and advocacy for individuals living with mental health conditions, including those who are neurodivergent.

3. The Arc - The Arc is a national organization that advocates for and supports individuals with intellectual and developmental disabilities (IDD), including autism, Down syndrome, and cerebral palsy.

4. The Best Plants For Earth – Although relatively new, The Best Plants For Earth focuses on supporting people from all forms of life to become healthier by becoming informed of the foods you eat, the products you buy, and the connections of organizations and support groups to further deepen your knowledge of those issues. Founded in 2021, The Best Plants For Earth started by selling environmentally friendly, plant themed, or plant-based retail products and clothing. In 2023 they opened their Microgreen Division which grows, sells, and delivers Organic and Fertilizer & Pesticide Free Microgreens to North Alabama to help increase the health of community members. They're focus with Microgreens is to help everyone experience the better taste, nutrients, and health benefits of Microgreens. One of the most prominent bioactive compounds found in their Microgreens is called Sulforaphane and is the main compound found only in such concentrated portions the growth cycle of Microgreens which gives their Microgreens their health benefits. They also started a Community Program called "Clean It Decatur!" Which brings community members together to pick up litter and gain knowledge or recycling

and other environmentally beneficial practices for trash.

HELPLINES AND HOTLINES:

1. National Suicide Prevention Lifeline: 1-800-273-TALK (1-800-273-8255) - Text 988- This hotline provides free and confidential support for individuals in crisis, including those who are experiencing thoughts of suicide.

2. Crisis Text Line: Text HOME to 741741 - The Crisis Text Line offers free, 24/7 support via text message for individuals in crisis or experiencing emotional distress.

3. SAMHSA National Helpline: 1-800-662-HELP (1-800-662-4357) - The Substance Abuse and Mental Health Services Administration (SAMHSA) helpline offers confidential assistance and referrals for individuals and families facing mental health and substance use disorders.

GLOSSARY OF TERMS:

1. Autism Spectrum Disorder (ASD): A developmental disorder characterized by challenges in social communication and interaction, as well as restricted and repetitive behaviors and interests.

2. Attention-Deficit/Hyperactivity Disorder (ADHD): A neurodevelopmental disorder characterized by difficulties with attention, hyperactivity, and impulsivity.

3. Dyslexia: A learning disorder characterized by difficulties with reading, spelling, and writing, often due to challenges in phonological processing.

4. Dyscalculia: A learning disorder characterized by difficulties with mathematical concepts and calculations.

5. Dysgraphia: A learning disorder characterized by difficulties with writing, including handwriting and written expression.

6. Dyspraxia: A developmental coordination disorder characterized by difficulties with motor coordination, planning, and execution of movements.

7. Tourette Syndrome: A neurological disorder

characterized by involuntary motor and vocal tics that typically emerge in childhood.

8. Intellectual Disability: A neurodevelopmental disorder characterized by limitations in intellectual functioning and adaptive behaviors.

9. Sensory Processing Disorder (SPD): A condition where individuals have difficulty processing and integrating sensory information from the environment, leading to sensory sensitivities or sensory-seeking behaviors.

10. Specific Language Impairment (SLI): A developmental disorder characterized by difficulties with language comprehension and expression, despite normal cognitive abilities.

11. Auditory Processing Disorder (APD): A condition where individuals have difficulty processing auditory information, leading to challenges in understanding spoken language.

12. Nonverbal Learning Disorder (NVLD): A neurodevelopmental disorder characterized by difficulties with nonverbal communication, visual-spatial skills, and social interaction.

13. Executive Function Disorder (EFD): A condition where individuals have difficulties with cognitive processes such as planning, organization, decision-making, and self-regulation.

14. Oppositional Defiant Disorder (ODD): A behavioral disorder characterized by persistent patterns of defiant, disobedient, and hostile behavior towards authority

figures.

15. Selective Mutism: A anxiety disorder characterized by the inability to speak in certain social situations, despite being capable of speech in other contexts.

16. Rett Syndrome: A rare genetic disorder that primarily affects females, characterized by developmental regression, loss of motor skills, and stereotypical hand movements.

17. Fragile X Syndrome: A genetic disorder characterized by intellectual disability, behavioral challenges, and physical features such as a long face and large ears, caused by a mutation in the FMR1 gene.

18. Williams Syndrome: A genetic disorder characterized by intellectual disability, distinctive facial features, and a friendly and sociable personality.

19. Angelman Syndrome: A genetic disorder characterized by developmental delays, intellectual disability, speech impairments, and a happy disposition, caused by a deletion or mutation in the UBE3A gene.

20. Prader-Willi Syndrome: A genetic disorder characterized by hyperphagia (excessive eating), intellectual disability, behavioral problems, and low muscle tone.

*These are just a few examples of neurodivergent disorders, and it's important to note that everyone may experience these conditions differently, with a unique combination of strengths and challenges...

Sources:

- Silberman, S. (2015). NeuroTribes: The Legacy of Autism

and the Future of Neurodiversity. Penguin Books.

- Prizant, B. M. (2016). Uniquely Human: A Different Way of Seeing Autism. Simon & Schuster.

- Grandin, T., & Panek, R. (2015). The Autistic Brain: Helping Different Kinds of Minds Succeed. Mariner Books.

- Autism Speaks. (n.d.). Retrieved from www.autismspeaks.org

- ASAN. (n.d.). Retrieved from www.autisticadvocacy.org

- NAMI. (n.d.). Retrieved from www.nami.org

- The Arc. (n.d.). Retrieved from www.thearc.org

-National Suicide Prevention Hotline (n.d.). www.suicidepreventionlifeline.org

- Crisis Text Line. (n.d.). www.crisistextline.org

- SAMHSA National Helpline. (n.d.). www.samhsa.gov

References:

- Hollocks, M. J., Lerh, J. W., Magiati, I., Meiser-Stedman, R., & Brugha, T. S. (2019). Anxiety and depression in adults with autism spectrum disorder: A systematic review and meta-analysis. Psychological Medicine, 49(4), 559–572.

- Hirvikoski, T., Mittendorfer-Rutz, E., Boman, M., Larsson, H., Lichtenstein, P., & Bölte, S. (2016). Premature mortality in autism spectrum disorder. The British Journal of

Psychiatry, 208(3), 232–238.

- Nigg, J. T. (2013). Attention-deficit/hyperactivity disorder and adverse health outcomes. Clinical Psychology Review, 33(2), 215–228.

- Doren, B., Gau, J. M., & Lindstrom, L. E. (2012). Handbook of self-determination research. Springer Science & Business Media.

- Happe, F., & Vital, P. (2009). What aspects of autism predispose to talent? Philosophical Transactions of the Royal Society B: Biological Sciences, 364(1522), 1369–1375.

- Nicolaidis, C., Raymaker, D., McDonald, K., Dern, S., Boisclair, C., Ashkenazy, E., Baggs, A., & Kapp, S. (2011). Collaboration strategies in nontraditional community-based participatory research partnerships: Lessons from an academic–community partnership with autistic self-advocates. Progress in Community Health Partnerships: Research, Education, and Action, 5(2), 143–150.

- Dabelea, D., Mayer-Davis, E. J., Saydah, S., Imperatore, G., Linder, B., Divers, J., Bell, R., Badaru, A., Talton, J. W., Crume, T., Liese, A. D., Merchant, A. T., & Lawrence, J. M. (2014). Prevalence of type 1 and type 2 diabetes among children and adolescents from 2001 to 2009. JAMA, 311(17), 1778–1786.

- Americans with Disabilities Act (ADA), Pub. L. No. 101-336, 104 Stat. 327 (1990).

- Individuals with Disabilities Education Act (IDEA), 20 U.S.C. §§ 1400 et seq. (2004).

- Autism Collaboration, Accountability, Research, Education, and Support (CARES) Act, Pub. L. No. 116-94, 133 Stat. 3038 (2019).

-Moller, R. (2023, October 10). Autism myths and stereotypes. Above & Beyond ABA Therapy. https:// www.abtaba.com/blog/autism-myths-stereotypes

- Ennaglobal. (2023, November 9). How to create a neurodiversity-friendly office environment. Enna. https://enna.org/how-to-create-a-neurodiversity-friendly-office-environment/

- Explore synergy of disability and Mental Health. ConnectAbility Australia. (2023, December 16). https://www.connectability.org.au/the-intersection-of-disability-and-mental-health/